LEARN TO DRAW
ANGRY BIRDS™
SPACE

ROVIO™ BOOKS

TABLE OF CONTENTS

THE STORY OF ANGRY BIRDS SPACE

IN SPACE, NO ONE CAN HEAR YOU OINK!

The Angry Birds have always guarded their precious eggs against the attacks of the egg-hunting Bad Piggies, but one day a totally new menace appears on Piggy Island.

A huge wormhole opens in the sky and a bird resembling an ice cube storms through the hole. It is the Ice Bird, and he is trying to protect his Eggsteroid—a magic egg-shaped asteroid. Soon a huge metallic arm reaches out from the wormhole, and everyone on the island hears the booming evil laughter of the Space Pigs.

The Space Pigs scoop up both the Eggsteroid and the Eggs into the looming darkness. The birds immediately rush after their eggs, flinging themselves into the wormhole just before it disappears. Suddenly, the Angry Birds find themselves in a strange space universe! Their appearance has changed and they are geared up like superheroes.

Before realizing what happened, they see their enemy with their eggs! Can you guess what they did next?

TOOLS & MATERIALS

Before you begin drawing, you need to gather the right tools. Start with a regular pencil, an eraser, and a pencil sharpener. When you're finished with your drawing, you can bring your characters to life by adding color with crayons, colored pencils, markers, or even paint!

drawing pencil and paper

colored pencils

paintbrush and paints

eraser

felt-tip markers

sharpener

HOW TO USE THIS BOOK

Professional artists draw characters in steps. The key is to start with simple shapes and gradually add the details. The blue lines will help guide you through the process.

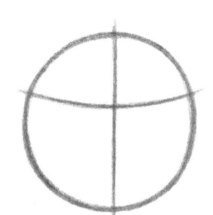

1 First you'll draw guidelines to help position the character's features.

2 Next you'll add the details, step by step.

3 When you finish adding the details, erase your guidelines. Then darken your final sketch lines with a pen or a marker.

SIZE CHART

Super Red   Lazer Bird   Space Bomb   Ice Bird

Corporal Pig   Foreman Pig   King Pig   Big Bork

SUPER RED

Super Red is the leader of the Space Flock. He trusts in his *SuperSpace Mask,* which has multiple features from tracking devices to a super-zoom. Red will not rest until he finds the missing eggs.

3

2

1

SUPER RED'S EXPRESSIONS

Screaming

Colliding

Cheering

Blinking

Flying

Looking Right

Jumping

15

LAZER BIRD

Lazer Bird is one of the fastest things in the universe when he uses his superpower, the *Ultimate Lazer Rush.* Lazer Bird is the joker of the group and, being a little impatient, he often gets the flock into trouble.

SPACE BOMB

Space Bomb wears a superhero cape with a shining Angry Birds Egg Brooch attached to it. He loves using his superpower, *Shock Bang,* which destroys unwanted objects and sends them to outer space.

ICE BIRD

Ice Bird is the coolest of the birds. His super-power, *Deep Freeze Attack,* turns different elements into ice. With icicles for a plume and tail, he has the appearance of an ice cube. The Angry Birds are helping Ice Bird to get his Eggsteroid back from the Space Pigs.

3

2

1

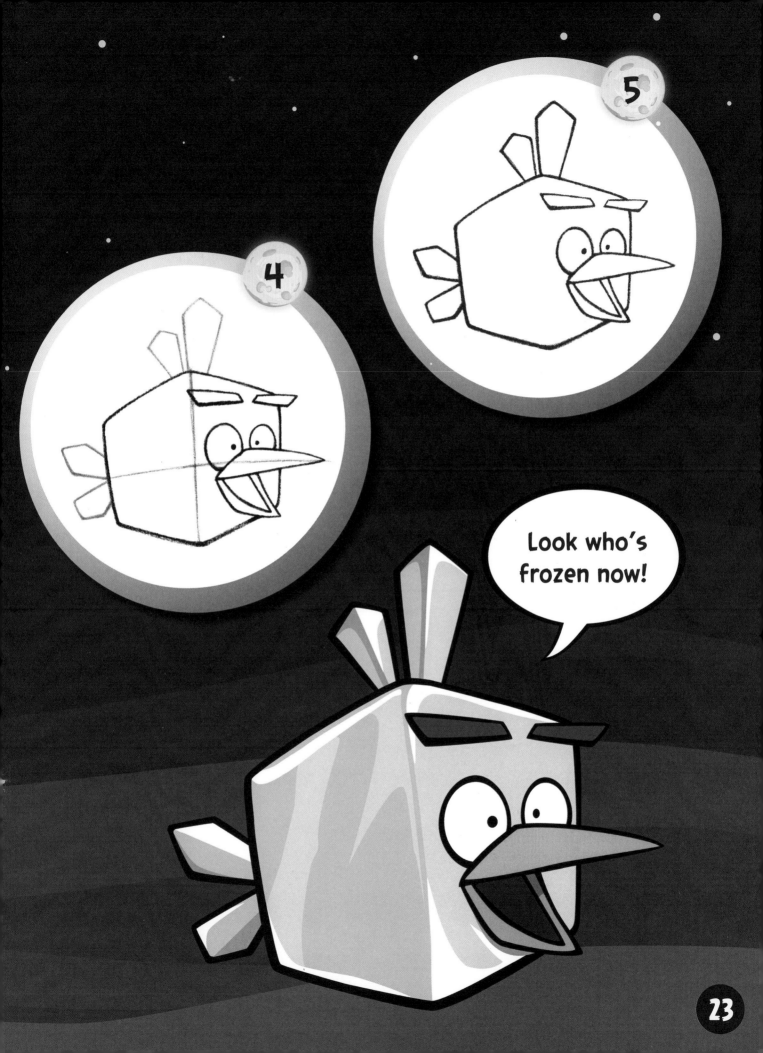

BIG BORK

This Space Pig has large green spots on his skin and facial features that are too small for his huge head—he's simply MASSIVE! But that's pretty much the scariest thing about him. Generally kind and harmless, Big Bork only frightens others because of his size.

3

2

1

CORPORAL PIG

As commander of the Space Pig army, the Corporal Pig wears a shiny, metal antenna attached to his steel helmet. However, this leader is not to be messed with; he's known for being a bully who rules with an iron fist!

FOREMAN PIG

The Foreman Pig manages the building of contraptions and structures, and he considers himself the ultimate expert—though nobody else agrees! He's usually grumpy and can often be heard muttering to himself that life was better back in the old days.

SPACE KING PIG

In Space, the King Pig often adapts his choice of headgear and signature gold, jewel-encrusted crown to the climate and scenery. Though he is the ruler of all pigs, he is known for being lazy and immature.

Can we get some jewels on this tin foil?

31

THE END

Now that you've learned the secrets to drawing the superhero Angry Birds and Space Pigs, create your own out-of-this-world adventures— without ever leaving planet Earth! All you need is a pencil, paper, and your own imagination!